My True Life Story

Growing Up in the Appalachian Mountains

Mazell Shepherd Miley

Copyright © 2021 Mazell Shepherd Miley
All rights reserved
First Edition

PAGE PUBLISHING, INC.
Conneaut Lake, PA

First originally published by Page Publishing 2021

Cover Picture

The picture on the cover is my dad, James "Black Hawk" Shepherd. The gun he is holding is the old gun that sat back of our cabin door. Mom used the gun to scare the men that would bring moonshine.

ISBN 978-1-6624-3721-2 (pbk)
ISBN 978-1-6624-3722-9 (digital)

Printed in the United States of America

I wish to dedicate this book to these wonderful people who lived in the Appalachian Mountains, my parents and grandparents, my schoolmates, and the wonderful people I worked with long ago.

My mother prayed a lot when I was growing up. If I'm very still at night and very quiet when I go to bed, I can still hear her prayers.

Prologue

Mom and Dad, you were my shining light, you kept me from straying day and night. You helped keep me strong, so I would do no wrong.

Mother, I wanted to keep you a little longer. We watched over you day and night.

Until at last, with broken hearts, we had to say goodbye. Just a few miles in a cold lonely grave

Lies the body of dear mother who we could not save.

God was with you while you suffered, he knew you had your share.

He gently closed your eyes and took you in his care.

Dear reader,

    This book you are about to read is about a hard-working, honest family. A widowed mother that raised her family of six children alone and never asked for help. A family that has been let down by the legal system. We have all been taught to be law-abiding, good citizens. When one of us was accused of a crime, we put our faith in the legal system. Only to find innocent people can spend thousands of dollars and end up not getting the justice and rights granted by the Constitution of the United States and the State of Ohio. These Constitutions are founded upon a fundamental belief of God.

    My son has paid with his money, sweat, but mostly his health and life again and again for being a friend to these families. They have robbed him of his self-respect. The courts have taken a part of his life and livelihood.

Introduction

This is a true story about a family that did live in the Appalachian Mountains of Eastern Kentucky. This is my story about a community, a coal company, and the proud people I remember. I was born there, lived and worked there, and buried friends and family there. I started this story a long time ago. Now I have the time to finish it.

My dad, James "Black Hawk" Shepherd, was born on October 1879 on Brushy in Magoffin County. He was the son of William "Brushy Bill" and Elizabeth "Hale" Shepherd. They lived in an old log cabin, one room was their bedroom and living room. Heating was done with a fireplace that burned coal and wood, and their cookstove also used coal and wood. Dad had seven brothers and six sisters. Their farm consisted of six hundred acres, a lot of hills and trees.

When my dad was very young, the Indians came and took him, his brother Sam, and their friend, Tom Cole, to the Indian reservation in Oklahoma. My dad stayed and got his schooling, Tom and Sam left and came home. They could not read or write, but my dad could. All my grandma Elizabeth's life and her daughter feared of being sent to the Indian reservation. They were very quiet about their lives and their ancestors, and little can be found. Dad always said his family was from the Cherokee tribe.

My dad was married first to Willie Hale. Her husband was shot and killed for the change in his pocket. Dad and Willie had seven children—Chandler, Vernie, Chess, Babe, and Sage. The two other children, Haley and Ad, died at childbirth.

My mother's father, my grandfather—Riley Shepherd—talked my mother Rhoda into marrying my dad and caring for his children.

Our cabin at the mouth of Lick Fork. On the left is the kitchen. Dad would sit on the end of the porch on the right. The washstand was outside the kitchen door.

Chapter 1

My mother, Rhoda Shepherd, married my dad, James "Black Hawk" Shepherd, in the year 1921 in Floyd County. James had a log cabin in Lick Fork—now David—in Floyd County, where he was living with his first family. His older sons had left to live in Greenwich, Ohio. His youngest son was two years old when he married my mother, Rhoda. They were married for two years before their first daughter, my sister Grace, was born. They had two more daughters and six boys—Grace, Mazell, Daley, Floyd, Riley, Diamond, William, Thomas, and Dial. My mom was twenty-one and my dad was forty-one years old when they were married.

There was no doctor close by. So when a woman was going to have a baby, she would send an older child to fetch Molly. I guess she would be called a midwife now. When the time came, my mother would send one of the oldest children to fetch her. Usually, it would be me. She lived about two miles away. I would run across her old orchard to her house. I was at the end of the orchard. A lot of the limbs were dead on the apple trees and sometimes I had to run to her in the middle of the night. I felt the limbs were reaching out to me as I ran past. Then I had to wait until I could get my breath before I could talk to her. She knew without me telling her that Mom was having a baby. Molly was also the one that taught Mom about the wild greens and wild tea that Mom would pick to help us eat and be well. She would let us pick apples from that old orchard. She would help Mom when one of was sick. We all loved Molly.

There was a large rock that hung on a cliff there on Brushy, making a sort of cave. When school was taught on Brushy, some of the children did learn to read and write on slates there. During the Civil War, people would hide their animals in the cave to keep them safe. Some people said men would gamble there at night.

Grandma Elizabeth was a very private person. She rarely talked about her life. She resembled an Indian with high cheekbones. She said that she was Cherokee Indian and several of her friends were taken on the Trail of Tears. She talked of people who lived in cabins with dirt floor and that they burned feathers around the perimeter of the cabin to keep the wolves from digging into the cabin. There were rumors of the older people hiding pieces of gold in their cabins, but none was ever found.

The reason Dad was not home a lot was because he was always visiting someone or his mother in another county. Some of the people he knew made moonshine and they would give him a bottle. He would not be able to walk home then. One time, I remember Mom and I went to Grandma Elizabeth's to find him. I wasn't very old, maybe four or five. We had ridden our gray mule, Nig. He was a very stubborn mule. Mom sat me on a big rock because Nig had broken loose from us. I was getting worried when I saw Mom coming up the hill leading Nig, she had not found Dad. It was getting dark, and we needed to get across the hill to home. There were no lights and when the sun went down, it was dangerous to be outside. Dad eventually came home.

Around this time, several large men came to talk to Dad. They were sitting on the porch and were drinking out of a jar. When they would talk to my dad, they kept calling him Dad. I could not understand. When they left, I asked Mom who they were, and she said they were my half-brothers. I couldn't understand how someone could be a half of a person. Mom explained that Dad had children from a first marriage, and they had a different mother who died.

We lived in a log cabin. It had two outside doors, one going into the kitchen the other into a large bedroom and sitting room with a large fireplace that heated the cabin. We burned coal and wood. One bedroom off the kitchen had four double beds and the other bedroom/sitting room had three double beds. The kitchen had a large cupboard, a stove that burned wood and coal, a long table with chairs where we ate and did our homework by a coal oil lamp. The porch off the kitchen held a washstand where we would wash up before going inside. Mom always had a bar of homemade soap and a pan of water there for us to use. A fence of rough boards surrounded our yard and garden. There wasn't grass but Mom would plant hollyhocks to give our yard some color. She would use a washboard to wash our clothes and hang them on a line in the yard. It was hard to get the clothes to dry in the winter.

This picture was taken in our yard at the cabin. I am on the left side of the picture, my younger sister Daley is on Mom's lap, and Grace is on the right.

Our school on Licking. Back row, third child is Grace Shepherd; last child by door is Mazell Shepherd. Middle row, first girl is Daley Shepherd.

We had a small tunnel in the hill behind the cabin. It was my sisters and my job to go in the tunnel with a pick to get coal for the kitchen stove and the fireplace since we were the oldest. We would carry firelights to see, one of us would hold the stick while the other would use the pick to loosen the coal. The chunks of coal we put in a burlap bag and carried home. Dad had placed posts on the sidewalls, and we were very careful not to touch or jar them. Water would run down the sides and along the floor, keeping the tunnel cold. We would store our milk and butter in there. We were always dirty and black when we were done.

Mom always had a large garden where we grew just about everything we needed. We had a gray mule that Mom would hitch the plow to so we could plant the garden. That old gray mule would get mean and if Mom or Dad weren't in sight, he would try to bite us. Dad had bought a young gray mule to help plow. He was different than Nig; he was slower, and we could pet him and not be afraid. In the fall harvest, we would can and dry the vegetables we grew. We had hens and one rooster. I didn't like him; he was mean and liked to make us run. Our shepherd dog was a good watchdog. He always slept or the porch, and we spoiled him. He died of old age.

We planted corn and Dad would grind it in the grist mill he had. Our neighbors would bring their corn by wagon and horseback and Dad would grind it and keep a part for the pay. He had a store where he sold ground corn, dried corn, flour, and jar of honey. He kept a record of the people who owed him money. Sometimes, they could not pay or would take trade, and some would trade for moonshine. Those people Mom would scare off with the old gun she kept behind the cabin door. We also planted cane for molasses. The mules were hitched to a long arm and went in a circle and the juice would drip in a pan. Then was boiled down to be thick and poured into jars. It was hard work. The fun time would be when we were making molasses. When school let out, Dad would make all the kids a paddle so they could eat some of the foam from the trough. Dad also had four beehives. He would rob the bees for the honey and never get stung. We always seemed to get stung, and Mom would make a vinegar and baking soda slurry and put on the sting.

Most of the time, my dad was not home. He would walk to his parents' home, sometimes he would ride Nig. Sometimes he would stop where he knew he could get a jar of moonshine. Many times, he would drop the reins and tell Nig to go home. Mom would bring him in and make sure he would eat.

We walked about a mile to school. The school sat between our cabin and Molly's. It was a one-room building with clapboard siding, a door in the middle and a flagpole to the right. We would pledge allegiance to the flag every morning before going inside. Mr. Ellis Hale was our teacher. He would ring a cowbell for us to begin our day. He was a strict teacher and didn't put up with foolishness. He would hit the desk with a ruler and scare us. There was a potbelly stove that used coal and wood to keep us warm. We took turns keeping the fire burning. But it seemed some us were always cold in the winter.

My mother raised eleven of us in poverty, but I didn't know we were poor until about the fifth grade. My hair was always washed and braided, my clothes were clean and mended. Mom would not cut me and my sisters' hair. There were times we would get lice from the other girls. She would have to use kerosene on our hair and scalps then use her homemade soap and comb the lice out. I know she was tired by the time she had the three of us done. The boys always had their hair short and didn't go through the lice treatment. She made our dresses on a treadle sewing machine. If we had extra vegetables or eggs, Mom would hitch the mules to an old wagon and go to Prestonsburg. She would take the money from the produce and buy material to sew for our clothes. Vernie would always get a new dress out of the material. Mom would be sewing the new dress and Dad would remind her she had three other little girls. Mom would answer him that Vernie was older and should have nice things. She would sew our dresses out of what was left.

Usually, when Mom would leave, Dad would not be there either. Our older half-sister was supposed to take care of us. She was mean and we would hide in the woods. We would not have anything to eat the whole time until Mom got home. Some Saturdays, Dad would hitch up the mules to the wagon and my older sister and I would go to Howard Branch to peddle extra vegetables, eggs, and chickens. We would leave early in the morning and around noon, we would have sold half of our load. Dad would go in the store and buy bologna and crackers for our lunch. About 4:00 p.m., we would be ready to go home. By then, someone would have slipped him a jar of moonshine and he would be asleep in the back of the wagon. He would just say give the mules the reins, they knew the way home. The last time I went with Dad, Mom was up and worried, it was already dark. Mom was always there. I was blessed with a mother that never changed. As I grew older, I realized what an extraordinary person she was. I have always tried to live up to the example she had set.

The salt lick Floyd found

Left to right:
All six brothers—William, Diamond, Riley, and Floyd
Mom with youngest son, Dial; Tom in
our yard at David, Kentucky

Chapter 2

The last time my sister and I went looking for my dad, Mom somehow knew he would be walking the same road back through the woods from Brushy. She fixed my sister and me two firelights to hold. They were pine branches with rags and set on fire. They were used to go into caves to dig for coal. It was getting dark and cold enough that it had snowed a little. We had walked about eight miles, ready to go across the big hill when we heard him. Dad had fallen and could not get up. We got on each side of him and got him up and held to him all eight miles back home. Dad did get better about drinking moonshine after that.

We had to carry all the water we used. From the well, for drinking and cooking and from the creek, for washing clothes. Before school, we had to feed the animals and milk our two cows and walk the mile to school. Mr. Hale rode a horse to school, there were no cars, the roads were in pretty bad shape. Sometimes, we would see a wagon drawn by mules, but mostly, people on mules or horses. If you needed a doctor, you would have to send someone to Prestonsburg, and he would ride a horse to you.

My brother, Floyd, became sick. He was about four years old. Mom said it was the whooping cough. Mom had him in a baby bed; he was losing weight and had a high fever that lasted many days. She would use a rag soaked in vinegar and cool water to lay on his head to bring the fever down. Floyd laid a long time. We had good neighbors, and some would come and sit with Floyd so Mom would have a break and rest. Dr. Archer came from Prestonsburg to tend to

Floyd. He told Mom because of the high fever, not to send him to school, that his brain could not take schooling. So Mom taught him at home. He could add numbers and could read some and sign his name. After Floyd got well, a man named Alka Davis asked Mom if Floyd could ride with him picking up garbage. Floyd then learned the hollers and names of people around Lick Fork. Everyone knew Floyd and he loved to watch the trains. Some of the engineers would stop and give him a short ride in the engines. They would drop him a short way from home and he would find his way back. One evening, he told us he found a salt lick when he was walking home. He said he would take us to see it. The salt was running through the water. I told him about Daniel Boone finding it before him.

When I was about eight years old, we had a terrible rainstorm; it had rained for several days and the creek behind our house was beginning to go over the banks. When I got home after school that evening, I had to get the animals across the creek and in the barn. The water was running really fast. I was determined to get the two milk cows, our bull, and two mules across the water and in the barn. The water pulled me down, but I caught a limb and pulled myself out. The animals made it across and waited for me on the other side. I was always afraid of water after that.

At the same time, my sister Gracie and I got a job with Norman and Gracie Shepherd hoeing corn. We walked about three miles carrying our hoes, worked all day in the fields, and walked home. We were paid $.50 a day.

Chapter 3

My best friend was Ora Lee Shepherd. She lived at the base of the hill where Dad would walk over to go to his mother. Ora Lee lived with her mom and dad—Tommie and Dave Shepherd—a sister, and brother. We would walk together to school and home, talking and laughing. She was a little older than I was. She was dating Roland Shepherd. Her dad did not approve of Roland.

The morning of October 3, 1939, Peggy Shepherd, Roland's mother, told us Ora Lee had died. She had been eating an apple and died under her bed. She had been late getting home the night before. Mom did not let us go to her funeral. I know they made her a pine box to be buried in. Many years later, I was in Frankfort, Kentucky, and went to the cabinet of records and asked for a copy of her death certificate. The woman who handed me the certificate said she was a true Snow White. She died eating an apple. I still miss her laugh and smile.

The first funeral I remember was Malcom Shepherd's. He was my Grandpa Riley and Grandma Donna's son. He was born on July 18, 1924, just fifteen days before me. He would walk the nine miles to see us. One time, when our roads had just been fixed, he hitched a ride on a wagon. We were hoeing corn near the road, and he was singing "take a ride on a wagon." He died on August 28, 1940 at age sixteen. He was in the Prestonsburg Hospital with appendicitis. Dr. Archer was on another call and could not get there in time. Malcolm died in his mother's arms. He was buried on Brushy Bill Cemetery. He was so much fun, and we missed him for a long time. I think of him still.

Grace and me at Berea College

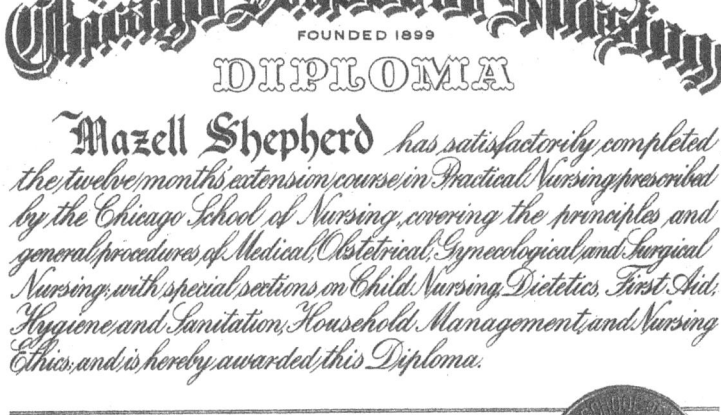

Mr. David Francis and his family. Mom received
Christmas cards for twelve years from them.

Princess Elkhorn Mining Co. in David, Kentucky. George Pickow, photo courtesy of the National Mining Hall of Fame and Museum, February 3, 2016

This photo by George Pickow dates back to the 1940s and shows old-style mining at the Princess Elkhorn Mining Co. in David, Kentucky. This was happening at a part of the mine where machinery could not be used. The photo is one of a series depicting coal mining in West Virginia and Kentucky that will soon be on display at the National Mining Hall of Fame and Museum. Born in 1922, Pickow was just at the start of his career when he took these photos. He is best known for thousands of album covers in which he portrayed folk, jazz, and pop music artists.

George Pickow photo courtesy of the National Mining Hall of Fame and Museum

The Clubhouse

The 110 steps leading to the Clubhouse.

Chapter 4

Our lives changed when Mr. David Frances came to our area in 1940. He was looking for coal. The research done showed the coal was there. The men he brought were Harry LaViers, G. J. Stollings, and E. J. Evans. These men were experienced in the mining of coal. My dad had gone with them to talk to our neighbors. They bought all our neighbors' land and mineral rights. They also bought my dad's land and lease, and the railroad would go through the backyard of our cabin near the creek. At this time, most of Dad's oldest children had moved to Greenwich, Ohio. Mr. Evans drove Dad and me to their homes so they could sign the agreement. It was the first time I had been in a car and the first time I had a milkshake. It was a long ride. Three of his children would not sign but two did, he sold anyway. We rode the bus home. Dad did not talk, he seemed to be thinking. Mr. Evans bought Jake and Peggy's acres, the mineral rights, all oil, gas, iron, stone, and standing timber. Most of the people who sold moved to Indiana. George and Katie Hale sold almost all their land to Henry LaViers, who was an employee of the company that wanted to start the Princess Elkhorn Mine. Coal would be profitable.

The men said that my dad, Black Hawk Shepherd, was a very unusual fellow to deal with; you had to take time, he wasn't to be pushed. When Mr. LaViers made the first approach to buy the right of way for the C&O railroad, he thought he had experience.

He realized these people had lived there all their lives and never had much money to spend. He was authorized to offer them $20 an acre. He said, "Well, I didn't buy any. I think it was because I sympathized with Black Hawk. I didn't plead my case strong enough." C&O finally bought most of it, I believe at $300 per acre.

Many people's lives changed when they began to take out the coal. Ours pretty much stayed the same. Dad was too old to work in the mines and my brothers were too young. Many men were hired to work in the mines, some from outside the area. The coal company built many houses for some of the workers and with the money earnest, many people began to fix or tear down older cabins. Our schoolhouse was a building that was torn down to build new housing. One building that was built was the Clubhouse. It was for the corporate men. Mr. Frances and Mr. Evans had taken an interest in my family, they respected my mom and dad.

My sister and I had graduated from school. Mr. Evans talked to my dad about sending my sister and me to Berea College. It took Mom longer to agree than Dad. She realized her help would be gone, but she also wanted the best for us. Mr. Evans drove us to Berea College. Our lives were changing fast. During this time, my half-sister and half-brother, who lived with us, moved to New London, Ohio. Mom was so proud of us. She wrote to us often. She wrote that she had taken in washing from the coal men. "I can send you girls some money. You can buy the things you need." We were there six months, everything was going good. We worked at the school part-time after classes. In a letter, Mom told us that Dad was not drinking as much and was staying home more that we were away.

My dad's daughter from his first family began to write letters to him, telling him she wanted what her dead mother left her. I guess that was the old log house we all lived in. Dad was walking to the post office until he got the first letter. After that, Mom would send one of us to walk the two plus miles. Dad cried a lot when he got the first letter. Mom made sure he never got another letter. There were more letters, but Mom would burn them, no one read them.

Then the bad news… Mom called our school, and the superintendent came to tell us our dad had died. May 7, 1941, he was sixty-two years old. The school released us to go home. Our Uncle Randel picked us up at the bus station in his Model T Ford. He could now drive to our house. The roads were built while we were away. Mom sat with us a long time, telling us what happened to our dad.

Mom said, "The three older brothers that lived in Greenwich, Ohio, came to visit their dad. They had stopped somewhere and had gotten a jar of moonshine. They sat with him and helped him drink the moonshine and then left to go back home. Your dad got up to go to bed and fell off the porch hitting his head. I put a cold washcloth on his head. He said he was all right and went to bed."

When my younger sister and Mom started breakfast the next morning and Mom went to wake him, he had died during the night.

Mom always took good care of Dad, just like she did all of us. She said he had quit grinding corn for all the neighbors and did not plant cane, also not going to make molasses anymore. He had worked some on WPA, but with us away, he had no help. Mom said the mine people are making money, you could see how our country has changed. We went from a peaceful living to a rich town. I could see our roads were good, lots of new cars on the road.

My dad's funeral was at home; his first children all came. A wagon and a team of mules carried him to Brushy, his old home place. He was buried there in the Brushy Bill Cemetery. His children never asked what happened to Dad. They never knew that they probably caused his death. My youngest brother was one year old when Dad died.

Dad had a pile of lumber, he wanted to build us a house. The men from the coal company took the lumber and built us a better house. We had electric for the first time. Our well was by the house now, about fourteen feet away. We still had to pull water up by the bucket, no running water. There was talk about renaming Lick Fork, and we heard they were thinking of calling it Black Hawk after my dad. Since he had died and Mr. Francis had done so much for the town, it was renamed David for Mr. Francis.

Chapter 5

I applied to the Clubhouse for a job a week after my dad died. The Clubhouse was a large house, the biggest house I had been in. There were seven bedrooms, bathroom, kitchen, living room, and dining room. I got the job, and my boss was Miss Ora Howard and Mr. David Francis. Mr. Francis had hired her to run the Clubhouse. I worked from 9:00 a.m. until long after dark. I did the cleaning, washed dishes, made beds, and helped Miss Howard prepare lunch and dinner. I also cleaned the foremen's houses down the road. There were 110 steps to enter the Clubhouse, and many days, I would go up and down the steps three times before walking home at night.

One evening, everyone had gone home for the weekend and a man rang the doorbell looking for Jim. I told him everyone was gone. He asked if I as Black Hawk's daughter. I told him yes and he left. That night, around 11:00 p.m., the next-door house was shot through. The Harmon family lived there, but no one was home. There were no streetlights and everything was really dark.

I also had to cook and wait on the men when Miss Howard went home to West Virginia on the weekends. The one part of my job I didn't like was standing in a corner of the dining room when the men were eating. I was to be close in case the men needed anything. I asked Miss Howard the next time she went home to get a bell set so when the men need something, they could ring the bell. That way, I could work in the kitchen and get home before dark. She never got the bell.

Many times, I would hear Mr. Francis ask Miss Howard to check on my mom to see if she needed anything. She told Mr. Francis she talked to Mom and that Mom had a big garden and lots of vegetables and lots of flowers. While I worked, Mom was still washing and ironing for the miners. She never told Mr. Francis that and she never talked to Mom. I worked seven days a week. The only things I remember getting from Miss Howard was a pair of used nurse's shoes I could not wear, some material for a dress, and a hat. I did not have time to sew a dress, and no time or place to wear a hat. Most of the time, I worked inside, but sometimes I would plant flowers and weed.

One night, I asked Mom if anyone paid her for my work.

She said, "No and remember, they built this house for us and we now have electricity."

I said, "But maybe Mr. Francis thinks I'm being paid." But it was dropped from our minds.

How I hated running home at night in the dark past the coal tipple and across the railroad tracks. My older half-brother did visit my mother after Dad died. He talked my mother into letting my older sister go with him to Greenwich, Ohio. He said she could get a good job and send money home. They had her to help clean house and babysit. No money was given to her to send home. They never let her have a day off to get a paying job.

Our youngest half-brother, I know he loved us all, he was very good to us. He lived with us growing up, he was little when his mother died. He was married now and living in New London, Ohio. One day, he went to his oldest brother where Grace was and said he was taking her for a ride. He had just bought a new car. He took her to a factory called C. E. Wards to get a job, and he helped her get a place to rent.

About this time, Mr. Francis was called to the service. World War II was having an effect on our small coal town. He would return to us as the president of the mining company. Mr. Francis found me working at the Clubhouse and said he would be gone for a few years. "Will you keep the home fires burning for me?" I did not say anything, he did not know Miss Howard like I did. Miss Howard gave me a week vacation. After working two years and nine months, I was due a vacation. I wanted to know what money looked like. I called my sister, she said her landlady and her would pick me up at the bus station in Norwalk, Ohio.

I got a job at C. E. Wards in New London making uniforms for our soldiers in World War II. I called Miss Howard at the Clubhouse to tell her I have a new job, I quit. Miss Howard started to cry and begged me to come back. She reminded me what Mr. Francis said about keeping the home fires burning. I know all this, but I needed a job to make money so I could help my mom. She needed a better life and I thought I could give it to her working in Ohio.

I was very unhappy sewing trousers. When the girl next to me sewed her finger, the blood was all over her machine and mine. It was time to look somewhere else to work. We had heard Westinghouse in Mansfield, Ohio, was hiring. Grace and I rode the train from New London, Ohio, to put in our application. I could not be hired until I turned eighteen, which was only a couple weeks later. The secretary was very nice and said she would hold my application until then. I was hired the week of my eighteenth birthday. We rented an apartment on High St. in Mansfield. Grace and I had been looking for a house to buy or rent in order to bring Mom and everyone together again. We found an old schoolhouse on O'Possum Run Rd., outside of Mansfield, to buy. Grace and her boyfriend rented an open bed truck and drove it to David to bring Mom and the rest to Mansfield. It was a good day when we were all together again. We all had to sleep on the floor with the quilts and blankets Mom brought from Kentucky. It was too far to walk to Westinghouse, so we paid a man $2 a week to take us and bring us home.

I know my mother went through a lot of pain leaving Kentucky, she had so many memories, good and bad. It took us a little time to furnish that old schoolhouse, but we did it. We were still looking for a bigger house closer in Mansfield where we could walk to work. We found a bigger house on Newton Place, just several blocks from work. We lived there until everyone grew up and were on their own.

One of the things Mom brought with her from Kentucky was the family Bible. Dad had written births and deaths of his first and second family in the Bible. We were moving in the house on Newton Place when Dad's oldest son—Chandler—came to the schoolhouse and wanted to borrow the Bible. Mom gave him the keys to our new house and told him the Bible was in the upstairs bedroom at the top of the steps on a shelf. She told him to put the keys under the chair on the front porch. He said he would bring the Bible back. Mom trusted him to do what he said. Many years later, I took Mom to see him. He was in the hospital, paralyzed. His wife was with him, he said his sister—Vernie—took the Bible and would not give it back. He died in 1982 and is buried in Greenwich, Ohio. It would not be until 2008 when we would see the Bible again. It was in terrible shape, the cover and many pages were missing, scribbles of crayon on pages, lots of damage. We found a gentleman in Willard, Ohio, to make a beautiful box for the Bible and sent it to the Magoffin Historical Society in Salyersville, Kentucky. It is there on a shelf for anyone to see. We also sent a large picture of Black Hawk for their wall. Their sidewalk has memorial bricks outside the pioneer village, and I had one put for Mom and Dad.

Chapter 6

After I raised my family of six children alone, my husband had died in 1970. I took my mom and took a trip back to my place of birth. I was shocked to see how awful everything looked. So many cars sitting about every place that did not run anymore, a lot of houses needing a lot of work. Mom had told me she saw in the *Floyd County Times* where David Francis had died. I had always known that he was the heart and soul of David, Kentucky—his namesake. It would take a lot of work to bring it back. I went to the Clubhouse, where I worked. There is a cemetery close by I wanted to see. I did talk to the woman who bought the clubhouse, she offered to let me go in and see a lot of memories. But I wanted to go to the cemetery, I never had time when I worked there. It was a short walk across the side yard where I worked with the flowers for Miss Howard.

I found the headstone of my best girlfriend, a large rock with her name. I found my dad's first wife and the graves of their two baby sons. My dad never talked about his first family members that died. I did not know where they were buried. I had worked at the Clubhouse almost three years. I spent a lot of time wondering about my dad. This was the cemetery he would walk past when he walked to Brushy, his birthplace, to see his mother. This was the walk where he would get moonshine. He had fallen near this cemetery and could not get up when my sister and I found him so long ago.

Mr. Francis did everything for the town of David. He built the clubhouse where I worked, the row of houses for workers, the church, the Boy Scout cabin, the school, the gymnasium, the doctor's office, the airfield where he landed his plane. The town grew and a water plant was built, a child care center, swimming pool, and craft center. Many people had a better life. He worked hard to provide for many people. He died in 1985, he lived in White Sulpher Springs in West Virginia. He died in Lewisburg after a long illness at the age of seventy. I believe the town is trying to come back as it has been sold for the third time.

My two girls and I made a trip to Brushy after my mom died to see the 19.9 acres my two brothers and I supposedly still own, everyone else had died. The county is still sending me land taxes. I have paid them now for twenty-five years. Some time ago, another coal company went on the land and took the timber and coal. After seeing how they destroyed the land, I went to the courthouse and told them the coal company said they bought everything from Branham and Baker Coal Co. before they filed bankruptcy. I will not be paying any more taxes on land I don't own. My dad's home place had been so much trouble for my mom her entire life.

Today, I looked through my mother's picture albums. I counted eleven Christmas cards from David Francis and family. I know he loved my family and helped us to have a better life. I have not found any of my school friends. When I write to them, a letter comes back from some of their grandchildren, telling me the classmate had died. I miss my hometown so much, a place where I was born and lived and worked when I was so young. Some time I have to go back and see it all again.

Bible belonging to James "Black Hawk" Shepherd with box.

My Grandma Rhoda

A true story told to me by my daughter, Carol.

Carol had just graduated from high school in the year 1967 and wanted to share her graduation present with her grandma. She wanted to take her to Kentucky. Every time in the past, it was always a rush trip and this time would be different. They were to be gone for a whole week and go everywhere Grandma wanted to go and see whoever she wanted to see.

The time they spent together was full of joy and laughter, also a little sorrow.

Grandma Rhoda was born Rhoda Shepherd on April 7, 1900, the daughter of Riley Shepherd and Lovella Hicks. She lived in Floyd County, Kentucky, most of her life and married James "Black Hawk" Shepherd of Magoffin, Kentucky, in 1922. Her cornbread, biscuits, and pies were the best. Every Thanksgiving, Carol couldn't wait to eat her oyster dressing and chicken dumplings. When Carol's son, Kenny, was born on Thanksgiving, we—mom and I—snuck a bowl of oyster dressing in the hospital.

Grandma died on June 29, 1994. Carol and I were with her when she died. She was in the hospital after having a stroke. We were hoping she would be able to talk to us again. She left a legacy of three daughters and six sons, many grandchildren and great-grandchildren.

The day their trip started was a warm sunny day, the sky was a bright blue, and the clouds were white and fluffy. Carol hadn't been driving long so they made many stops. They looked at quilts hanging on clotheslines beside roadside shops for sale. Grandma began to reminisce as the road began winding and sloping up and down. They were riding on the old Route 23 through Columbus, Ohio, and road crews were blasting out the hills for the new road. Grandma would talk of the relatives and friends we would stop and see, and maybe spend the night. They were ready for an adventure!

Their first overnight stop was in Prestonsburg, Kentucky, at an old hotel. It was late, and they were very tired and needed to rest. The room was large with high ceilings and a claw bathtub that was deep and inviting. Next morning, they awoke refreshed and ready.

Breakfast was in a diner that served eggs and biscuits with red-eye gravy. Carol had no idea what that was and it didn't sound very good. Grandma said it was made with ham drippings and black coffee. Carol wasn't that adventurous!

The first person they met was Essie Slone, one of Grandma's neighbors. They drove down a road made from the scraps from the coal mine. They visited for a while, sitting in the front room of her mobile home and ate lunch with her. She was very spry and had a lot of flowers around her home. Essie and Grandma talked of a cemetery called Sam Hale where they both had relatives buried. The decision was made, the cemetery was to be the next stop and Essie would go with them.

When they pulled in the drive and looked out the windshield, the hill where the cemetery was looked straight up, and Carol wondered how they would get a casket up to bury someone. The car was barely in park when Essie was out the door and halfway up the hill. Grandma and Carol followed at a much slower pace. They were concerned about running into snakes. Essie was at the top of the hill, struggling, with a large headstone that was made of concrete. They helped her right to the stone of her son, Jimmy, who was buried there. Essie said that Jimmy was in the woods squirrel hunting when a tree fell on him. She stood there a while, crying. She said that was the first time she had been there since his funeral.

The cemetery was being used as a pasture and cows were grazing around the headstones. Grandma stood not too far from Jimmy's grave and pointed to a spot to the left and said that was where her mother was buried. Grandma said she had not been on the cemetery since she was a child. They could not find a headstone for her mother and she told Carol they just put a large rock there to mark the spot. Grandma said that her mother, Lovella, was just thirty-five years old when she died, and it was a very sad time. She said it was hard for her, her sisters, and brothers without their mother. Her father, Riley, married shortly after Lovella died to Donna Shepherd. Grandma loved Donna as her blood mother and later when she married Black Hawk, Donna would become her sister-in-law.

Grandma spoke of the time when Floyd, her oldest son, developed whooping cough and the many hours she spent at his bedside holding him. Bathing him with apple vinegar towels, trying to get his fever down. She said, back then, very few children lived that had gotten sick. Many of the neighbors came to visit and helped her with Floyd. Many prayed for him. Grandma was a deeply religious person; she never boasted of being a Christian, but you had only to listen to her for a few minutes to know how deeply her love for God was.

Election day was a very important day and to hear Grandma talk of being able to vote made me proud that she always felt every vote made a difference. She said people came all over to the courthouse to vote. They would visit and talk politics. Grandma would bake gingerbread to take to town to sell, along with extra eggs and vegetables. Her gingerbread was shaped like a cookie, long and broad, that would melt in your mouth. Gingerbread with a cold glass of milk was a treat at Grandma's house. I still remember the taste and haven't been able to find it. Voting was a right that Mom impressed on Carol, and because of Grandma, Carol is a serious voter.

They would drive past where the cabin, Grandpa's store, and grist mill was. These buildings were long gone. Grandpa never had a moonshine still but knew where they were. Grandma didn't like him drinking but there wasn't much she could do about it. She told stories of scaring off the men who would bring him moonshine. She had an old gun behind the cabin door that she would stick out the door and threaten to shoot if they didn't leave. They would leave and she said it was a good thing they would leave because the gun wasn't in working order. They had a good laugh. Carol knew Grandma would have taken on an army to keep her family safe.

Grandma showed her where she had a large garden, where she would hoe corn, and where her mom, Mazell, would hoe corn with her sister for $.50 a day. Carol asked me how they worked so hard. "It was just what we did to live." Carol and Mom had a competition on who would have the first ripe tomato. It didn't matter when the gardens were planted, Grandma always won.

Many more places were on our trip. The overnight at Grandma's sister-in-law, Della, was an adventure. When she drove in the yard on a creek bed called Brushy, there was a log cabin, a real log house! Carol had never been inside a log house before. Della was a little bit of a woman, but she could hug you hard enough to break bones! She was Grandpa's younger sister and was also a twin. She was really happy to see them visitors were few. The house had no electricity, and it was getting dark. When they arrived at Della's house, she fixed them dinner. Carol said it was so good. She fixed green beans, corn, chicken, and corn bread. By the time dinner was over, it was dark. Della lit a coal oil lamp so they could see the bed. Carol had never slept on a feather bed before. When Grandma laid down, the mattress poofed up like a balloon, it was as if grandma disappeared. When Carol laid down beside Grandma, the mattress popped up between and they could not see each other. They laughed until they both fell asleep.

The next morning, after a breakfast of biscuits, gravy, bacon, and eggs, they set off for another cemetery. This cemetery was at the end of the creek bed road at the end of Brushy. It is named for William "Brushy Bill" Shepherd who was James "Black Hawk" Shepherd's dad. He had set aside this land for a family cemetery. There are many graves there. They had taken a large box of artificial flowers to place at graves. Grandma's husband and many of his brothers and sisters are buried there. The trip was coming to a close and after a short rest, they headed back to Mansfield.

Grandma had one more story to tell. She told Carol of leaving Kentucky with her children in a truck her two oldest daughters had sent for them. They didn't have many possessions, but she had been full of hope.

Grandma lived close to us and she and Carol were always close. I always thought how sad that my grandma didn't have a headstone. After Carol grew up and married, I thought of a plan to place a headstone. We ordered a headstone—a pink granite—and with Carol's husband's help, he carried and drag that headstone up the hill. Even though Rhoda didn't get to see the headstone, I know she would appreciate knowing it is there.

'Black Hawk' Shepherd Found Dead In Bed On Middle Creek

James "Black Hawk" Shepherd, familiar and picturesque figure in the Lick Fork section of Middle Creek during recent developments there of a new coal field, was found dead in bed at his home Wednesday morning. He was 91 years old.

A miller and one of his community's best citizens, Mr. Shepherd was well-known. He was featured in a recent Chesapeake & Ohio Railway Employes' Magazine story describing the Middle Creek rail and mine development, and his pseudonym had been suggested as the name of a postoffice sought for the new mining town.

Surviving him are his widow and several children. The body was brought here Wednesday to the Arnold Funeral Home for burial preparations. The body will be taken to Brushy Fork of Licking River, Magoffin county, his birthplace, for interment.

Added by R. Reed

Dad as a young man.

Dad shortly before his death.

The Ten Commandments Are Important to All

Today's problems stem from people not obeying the Ten Commandments. Justice has gone mad. Some people are in prison because the system forgot about God.

I believe the Ten Commandments should be in every courtroom, judges' chambers, and school classrooms. In most homes, both parents work. We need prayer back in schools so children will know it is wrong to kill, and they can trust in God.

The children need to know that Jesus is so good. Before he died, he took time to heal lepers, give sight to the blind, heal cripples, and raise the dead. This teaches that God takes the time to enter our lives with the power to save and heal.

I was raised in poverty and a large family. In the night, I could hear my mom praying. She would read to us from the Bible often. She slipped away on June 30, 1994; she was ninety-four years old. I know she is safe and happy in heaven. Her old Bible is so worn and faded, that I covered it with ribbon and flowers. A dove sits among the flowers and ribbon.

For Being Kind

Milton has been tossed from one prison to another. Not knowing what his course may be.

Like a ship lost at sea, his "friends" discredited him jealous, greed, and wanting money. Some friends he will never trust; they have brought shame on him. He was a humble person, he thought God blessed him for human kindness.

Myself with son, Milton

I Love My Country

I was sixteen years old when I worked at C. E. Wards. I made the soldiers uniforms. I was eighteen years old when I worked at Westinghouse. I riveted the tail cones for the fighter plane, P-47 Thunderbolt.

After my husband died, I raised our six children. My husband had started REACT and Toys for Tots. My one son is like his dad. He started like his dad, helping so many people. Two families—one lived here in Mansfield, the other lived in Lexington. They lied so much to him. Our judge also helped them; he did not listen to the truth. The justice system, or should I say, the lying system.

I had a lot of trouble when my husband was sick. I had Judge Lutz; he was a great judge. He helped me put the renter out. I thank him today and I pray for him yet. I know he is in a better place now.

My son has had his second heart attack. He now has five stints in his heart. So many times, he has called me saying, "Mom what am I doing here?" I knew he was still in shock. I told him his "friends" lied to him. "These are the people you helped so much."

The one prosecutor and the mother, making out on a picnic table at the bike path. Our three attorneys leaving the courthouse very upset. I was outside, they did not allow me there. One attorney said they did their best, they know he is innocent.

I told my son, "As soon as we can get you out, we will move."

He answered, "We can't move. Dad is buried here, so is Grandma and now, my sister and your brothers. We can't leave them here."

My answer to him, "If your dad was alive, he would move them all. Remember, he moved three houses."

Me (Mazell) riveting in the P-47 Thunderbolt tail cone.

WIKIPEDIA
Republic P-47 Thunderbolt

The **Republic P-47 Thunderbolt** was a World War II era fighter aircraft produced by the United States from 1941 through 1945. Its primary armament was eight .50-caliber machine guns, and in the fighter-bomber ground-attack role it could carry five-inch rockets or a bomb load of 2,500 pounds (1,103 kg). When fully loaded, the P-47 weighed up to eight tons, making it one of the heaviest fighters of the war. The P-47 was designed around the powerful Pratt & Whitney R-2800 Double Wasp engine, which was also used by two U.S. Navy/U.S. Marine Corps fighters, the Grumman F6F Hellcat and the Vought F4U Corsair. The Thunderbolt was effective as a short-to medium-range escort fighter in high-altitude air-to-air combat and ground attack in both the European and Pacific theaters.

The P-47 was one of the main United States Army Air Forces (USAAF) fighters of World War II, and also served with other Allied air forces, including those of France, the United Kingdom, and the Soviet Union. Mexican and Brazilian squadrons fighting alongside the USAAF also flew the P-47.

The armored cockpit was relatively roomy and comfortable and the bubble canopy introduced on the P-47D offered good visibility. A present-day U.S. ground-attack aircraft, the Fairchild Republic A-10 Thunderbolt II, takes its name from the P-47.[Note 1]

P-47 Thunderbolt

XP-47N flying over the Pacific during World War II

Role	Fighter-bomber
Manufacturer	Republic Aviation
Designer	Alexander Kartveli
First flight	6 May 1941
Introduction	November 1942[1]
Retired	1966, Peruvian Air Force
Primary users	United States Army Air Forces Royal Air Force French Air Force
Produced	1941–1945
Number built	15,636
Unit cost	US$83,000 in 1945[2]
Variants	Republic XP-72

Certificate of Appreciation

For Contributing to the
Rosie the Riveter/WWII Home Front
National Historical Park

Granted: 2004

Judy Hart
Judy Hart, Superintendent

THE NATIONAL WWII MUSEUM

IN GRATEFUL APPRECIATION FOR YOUR OUTSTANDING SUPPORT AS A CHARTER MEMBER OF THE NATIONAL WWII MUSEUM.

THIS IS TO CERTIFY BY UNANIMOUS VOTE OF THE BOARD OF TRUSTEES THAT THE NAME OF

MS MAZELL M MILEY
MANSFIELD, OH

Is hereby entered into the Honor Roll of
The National WWII Museum, New Orleans, Louisiana.
The Honor Roll shall be maintained in perpetuity at the entrance to the Museum,
and the names shall be listed with distinction on the Museum's website.

The Board further recognizes that the Charter Member named above
has contributed to the Museum in honor of:

MRS MAZELL SHEPHERD MILEY - Helped on the Homefront
MR JAMES W MILEY - WWII Veteran

The Museum wishes to express its heartfelt gratitude and appreciation to you
for demonstrating exemplary and steadfast loyalty to The National WWII Museum
as we embark on our mission to create a new national institution fully commensurate
with the size, scope and importance of World War II.

Certified this 24th day of March, 2018.

Stephen J. Watson, President and CEO

Epilogue

I started this book a long time ago. I have shared my story of my young life to the people of the Appalachian Mountains. I had to move to make a better life for my mother and family; although I loved the town called David and most of my people are there. I think of it still as my home. I am now ninety-five years old, and I have finished more books to publish—*No Time to Cry*, *A Sister's Rage*, and *Life Under Siege II*.

In the year of 1958, my mother and my daughter, Carol, and I went to see the old home place. First, we went to Brushy, my dad's home place. We took flowers, too, for the cemetery on the graves, walking around the many graves of friends and relatives.

Before my Grandpaw Brushy Bill died, he set a lot of acres aside for the large cemetery. My mom and myself wandered all over. Saw Tom Cole's name, the one the Indians took with my dad, and he was buried in our cemetery. I told Mom why didn't he live with some of us, mostly my Grandpaw Riley. "He lived with us and now he is buried with us too."

The people that takes care of the cemetery does a good job; it was beautiful and the graves were well taken care of. We also visited our relatives, Frankie and Valice, they live near the cemetery. As far as I remember, the preacher has church at the cemetery the last Sunday in August. We love to see everyone. When it is time for church, we make sure the roads are in good shape, just dirt roads.

We decided to go back to Middle Creek. There is a cemetery where my teacher is, and I believe all the hall people are buried there. We got to the cemetery. The hills seem straighter up and at the top, it was round. An old fence was around it. Most of the graves needed work, so overgrown, and we noticed an old headstone was uprooted. I pulled hard to get it to stand up, cleaned the dirt off. There was a picture of a man on it, it looked so new.

I saw my teacher's headstone; it was in good shape. Standing there, remembering all the good times and the bad ones too. I would be studying, and he would hit my desk with an old paddle.

We then walked down the hill to the car parked at the gate. I did talk to the lady in the big brick house, it was beautiful. She said she was just an in-law. I told her my grade schoolteacher was buried there. She said, "Did you enjoy seeing all the graves?"

We got to the car and decided to go to my home place used to be called Lick Fork, now called David, after my boss when I worked at the Clubhouse so long ago. As we got to the place that our old log cabin used to set, there was a trailer there. We went about sixty feet, looked up the hill, where the coal company took the lumber. They had built us a new house. There was a trailer there with lots of junk around, like it came from the trailer too. I had heard that my stepbrother, Babe, bought everyone out, his brothers and sister, for the land. The house did burn down and was sold to Norman Shepherd.

Babe and his wife had died, and they are buried up on the hill, above that house.

I did asked the man that lived there, "If you would mind if I go up and see their graves."

He said, "Just be careful, the hill is rough."

We held on to small trees as we climbed, pulling ourselves up to two headstones. It seemed as if no one is taking care of the stones; weeds trees were growing, bushes out of control.

The coal company wanted to know about the grave in the front yard beside the highway they built with the cement by the side of the road. My dad always said the man that is buried there was so big, they could not put him any place, so they buried him there. His wife and child are buried high up on the hill.

My mother's Grandpaw, my Great-Great-Grandpaw
He was a preacher

As a little girl, Mom would not allow us to go up there where the wife and child was buried. I think it has always been in my mind to find their graves very hard to find but we did find them.

After I found out I had stepbrothers and stepsisters, my dad and his first family did own the house that the coal company built for Mom and her family. We did not own anything. Dad, I guess, did not care enough for us to fix it so we could have a part of theirs; even the lumber Dad had there did not even belong to us, thinking that the moonshine he drank did not let him think of us.

We all loved our stepbrothers and stepsisters, we could have had a good life despite the ones that did not include us in their family. Sage and Chess, I know, did love all of us. They have all been dead for a long time now.

Now we just passed our old coal temple, remembering all the times I ran past that old temple, I never thought that one day, I would drive by it not running. Going by David's Craft Store, we loved going in there and seeing all the handmade crafts and quilts, just like what Mom made. So much to see. Now I drove up to the Clubhouse that had a big double gate, so I can't go up there. No one here to visit.

We had one more cemetery to visit. After a lot of driving, we found this cemetery. A woman came out of the house to talk to us.

Sometimes, my dad would talk to us about being out alone. He would scare us by telling stories about the Indians, how they dressed, wearing nothing, and sometimes he would talk about the creek that did cover everything on Sunday, June 27, 1910. This was a disaster for the family living on.

Now we just passed our old coal temple, remembering all the times I ran past that old temple, I never thought that one day, I would drive by it not running. Going by David's Craft Store, we loved going in there and seeing all the made crafts and quilts, just like what Mom made. So much to see. Now I drove up to the Clubhouse that had a big double gate, so I can't go up there. No one here to visit.

We had one more cemetery to visit, after a lot of driving we found this cemetery, a woman came out of the house to talk to us.

Sometimes, my dad would talk to us about being out alone. He would scare us by telling stories about the Indians, how they dressed, wearing nothing, and sometimes he would talk about the creek that did cover everything on Sunday, June 27, 1910. This was a disaster for the family living on.

Brushy Fork of the Licking River in Magoffin County, losing their lives was Roach Gearheart, Cynthia Hale Gearheart (daughter and only child), and Ramsom Stephens. They said that night, two storm clouds collided in the head of Brushy and Grassy Fork, releasing a storm in this area. A cloud burst. It had extreme lightning and rain. The rain just poured out of the sky, the stream rising at a rapid rate, covering all the low-lying ground, and the water begins to rise. Many lost their homes and everything.

A lot of schoolmates did live here in the holler across from our old schoolhouse. There was a family of twelve children we used to meet on their porch and sing, missing Della, Peggie Lou, Tommie. Wanting to visit where we hoed corn for fifty cents a day, they had lots of horses in the bottom of their property. With a cemetery on the side of the hill beside the house, it just did not look like anyone had lived there. The coal company made everything look rich for a while. Now the places look bad. I think when I was little and lived there, it did look better.

It was getting late. We will go to Prestonsburg, where we had a room for the night, this hotel is where we get a room every time we come to visit. We got back to the room and we began itching. I guess I got chiggers on the cemeteries. Up early, we got a free breakfast and a cup of coffee to go. I said when I get home, I will have to get to the doctor. I enjoyed this trip and will be glad to see Dr. Betty. Well, she did laugh at me, what was wrong with me, climbing hills with weeds. She gave me a shot for three days, one each day.

When and if we get another chance to go to my hometown, we will have two cans of spray. I don't like shots and need to sleep.

Brother Bill and I

1999 Shepherd Shrine
Magoffin Historical Society
In Salyersville, Kentucky

MY TRUE LIFE STORY

This is a true story about my mother that lived in the Appalachian Mountains of Eastern Kentucky, that was called Lick Fork. Now called David in Floyd County, an astonishing new growth to full maturity to sudden decay.

She lived there when the coal company came and when the coal company left. My mother washed clothes for the miners, and she raised all our vegetables that we ate. She always had a big garden. She made all our clothes on a treadle machine and did sew a lot for neighbor Peggy Shepherd and her two girls. In growing up, I always thought my mother was a hero, she would tell us that there was eleven of us children for Mom to take care of. She would always say, "Whatever you do, try to do it the best, not the best for everybody, but for yourself."

We did not have electric, we had outside toilet, and we washed our clothes on a board. We had good neighbors. When someone would get sick and needed help, the neighbors always was there to help.

Our country was one of the most beautiful areas in the world, to me, with the rugged mountains and sometimes muddy roads. My mother made life comfortable for all. She was born a small girl, she would work in the cornfields for her dad. Her dad talked to her. And when she grew up and got her to marry my dad, my dad was twenty years older than Mom, and he had small children. Grandpaw said he needed help raising them. Someone was always making moonshine in the woods on Brushy—my dad's home place. My mom was always ready with that old shotgun, that did not even work but they did not know that, and always scared them away. When my dad had too much moonshine, Mom would feed him no matter if it was not mealtime, so he would not get sick.

After my dad died in his sleep, we talked to Mom about coming to Ohio, she agreed to come. So we moved her here. My youngest brother was around three years old then. We found a house and bought it for Mom and the family so we could have a better life.

As the boys got older and could take care of themselves, Mom got a job at the hospital, taking meals to sick people. She had made a few friends and she loved her job. She never drove, so one of us always took her to work and picked her up. My mom never dated after my dad died. I guess she never had time even though we had all married and we still needed her help.

When my mother was ninety-three years old, she begin to make quilts every time I would stop by to see how she was doing she would have material in every chair and sometimes, she would hang them on the clothesline when they were finished. She began to have trouble with her eyes and had to give it up. I had been taking her meals and my one brother still lived with Mom.

When I went in, Floyd said something is wrong with Mom. She was sitting on the side of the bathtub, trying to talk. I called the ambulance for her and went to People's Hospital. Her doctor came in and said he was going on vacation to another country, he said it looks like she had a stroke. Then he said, "We are going to move her to the hospital in town." She began to vomit and they were short of help, I began to clean her up. The ambulance took her to Mansfield General, they did surgery on her left arm. They said there was a blood clot. She never gained consciousness. Mom died thirty days later, she had all her funeral arrangements made and paid for, and the church she had been going to had taken care of everything.

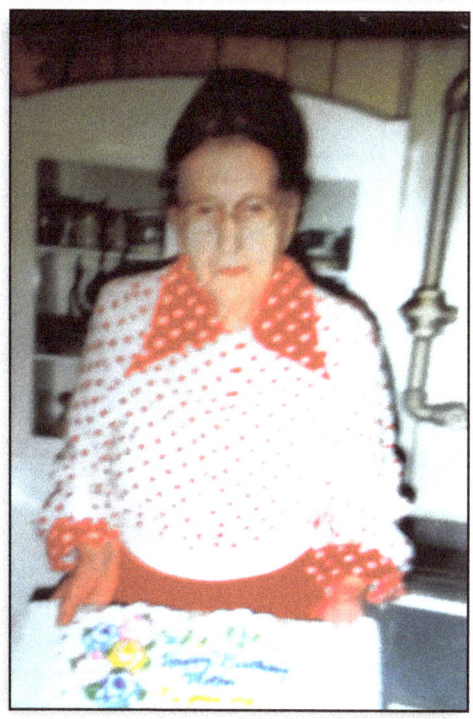

Mom's Bible is so worn out and fragile. I wrapped it in ribbon and a dove with a rose, set on top. Mom read this Bible a lot to all of us growing up. We all miss her so much.

For many of us, Lick Fork would always be named after the creek. During the mining community, it was given the name "David." No one remembered any formal announcement given to that change from Lick Fork to David. Perhaps it was just the parting of the letters signed "David" at the railroad tracks that transformed a quite Lick Fork to a busy active David. The real David that run the coal company. I did work for him for years ago. I know everyone at the Lick Fork, now his namesake David. We really did love him, he seemed to think a lot of my family. My mother, after she called me and talked about him, she said I have six boys but sometimes I think of him as a son. Then she called me and said in the *Floyd County* paper said that David had died. That's when the town of David begin to look bad. People was out of work. The mining of coal closed.

David was a place of beauty, clean, fresh, where all lived well, and everyone took pride in their community till the coal mine closed and David died.

About the Author

For her life now, Mazell is still gardening and taking care of her flowers and helping her daughter, Brenda, with her twenty cats (to count at this time). Her pawpaw trees are outdoing themselves, so many to take care of. She has always known that the pawpaw is a cancer fighter.

She has endured her mother's death and took care of her brother till he died. Some time, she has to go back to see her home in the mountains of Kentucky, that she loved so long ago.

Mazell has written four books, *Life Under Siege, My True Life Story: Growing Up in the Appalachian Mountains, Life Under Seige II, No Time to Cry, A Sister's Rage,* and *Life Under Siege III.*

CPSIA information can be obtained
at www.ICGtesting.com
Printed in the USA
BVHW021421080922
646570BV00014B/135